By Grand Central Station
We Sat Down and Wept

Poetry inspired by
Elizabeth Smart's
By Grand Central Station I Sat Down And Wept.

Devised and Edited by
Kevin Cadwallender
for Red Squirrel Press

Introductory poem
by
Sebastian Barker
From
'Guarding the Border': Selected Poems.
(Enitharmon 1992) Copyright Sebastian
Barker.

Red Squirrel Press

First published in the UK by
Red Squirrel Press
Po Box 219
Morpeth
NE61 9AU
www.redsquirrelpress.com

ISBN   978-1-906700-31-7

Printed by Martins the Printers
Sea View Works, Spittal
Berwick-upon-Tweed
TD15 1RS

Introduction

I first had the idea for this book in 2005 after I had re-read *By Grand Central Station I Sat down and Wept*. After having not read it for many years. I started to underline titles for poems with the idea of choosing ten to write a sequence of poems myself. I did write those poems but was never happy with them. Tucking the idea away in the back of my head I busied myself with other matters until 2010.

The impetus for this retrieval came when the poet Rob A. MacKenzie was doing an evening of poems by invited poets written from lines of Solomon's Song of Songs. It was a great event to which I contributed a poem.

After that I decided it might be a good idea to approach the Grand Central titles in the same way rather than hogging the lines to myself. I duly put up a note on facebook (ah the modern world!) to which I received a surprising, no, overwhelming response.

After a quick chat with the greatest managing editor in the history of small presses Sheila, whose support and enthusiasm for this and all my projects is unbounded like my gratitude to her and... we had a book.

Next I made a list of poets I would like to do it and most were generous with their time and talent.

I am indebted to Sally Evans, (another fabulous poetry spirit) who suggested I get in touch with Sebastian Barker and see if he would give the book his blessing, which I did and he did and also gave two poems he had written for his mother. I have used one but both poems were very beautiful and have a hymn like quality to them.

So thank you to both Sally Evans and Sebastian Barker.

The poems in this book are a response to lines selected and given by me and all poets responded magnificently with a mesmerising assortment of styles, subjects and imagination. It was a delight to edit and I still think I might be dreaming this. So thank you to the poets.

There is deliberately no contents page as this book is a browser, dip in and enjoy the eclectic mix from page to page.

Thanks also to Colin Donati for conversations on the subject and to Deborah Murray for her support in putting this together.

Lastly thank you to Elizabeth Smart for her inspirational book.

Kevin Cadwallender August 2010.

O Mother Heal Your Son

I fell asleep and dreamed a dream.
The world like a globe in night;
The sun shone like a golden beam.
The stars and planets too were bright.
Great galaxies like specks behind
Majestic space sublimely spun.
I searched the infinite of mind.
O mother heal your son.

I went where water laps the rock
And quiet pools greet storm-tossed fish.
I saw the Pleiades unlock
And diamonds spilling in a dish.
But heard the radar of the past
Booming like a hunter's gun:
The miracles of hope don't last.
O mother heal your son.

Through dusty vaults of books by floors;
By cherry blossom on new-mown grass;
Through flaps of mosques, cathedral doors;
And bridges summer students pass:
I searched the places where I'd known
Inspired, the air of vision stun.
Your death had turned them all to stone.
O mother heal your son.

The morning sky no brighter blue
Shocks on my inward brooding gaze.
The trees of early summer too
No greener in their fountains blaze.
The loves I have, dissolving night,
Persuade me like undoubting sun.
They prove, though wrong, their love is right.
O mother heal your son.

At night I watch the moon float by;
The curtains rustle in the breeze;
A cat is walking in the sky,
And nothing in myself agrees.
I rise and dress and make some tea
And drink it as the flashbacks run.
You love was always home to me.
O mother heal your son.

I take a book and find a page.
I cannot read the lucid text.
It is your battlefield with age,
Fresh corpses, where my own is next.
It breaks my heart to see you die
So nobly, every battle won
Now all are lost, for there you lie.
O mother heal your son.

The heaps of flowers rot on your grave.
The seasons change. My child appears.
The antique ecstasy of love
Drives the dynamo of years.
Time generates new life again.
The spark of sex: it's all begun.
No greater love knows greater pain.
O mother heal your son.

Sheep and lambs graze by the church.
Rooks are raucous in the elms.
In blue, a dazzling silver birch
The cornfield overwhelms.
I note the instinct to admire
Stoops with grief but soars to fun
Through which we parachute to fire.
O mother heal your son.

My shed by day looks calm but dark.
A sunbeam slants across the wall.
I take a chisel from the rack
And chip a mortise for a table.
The mallet's long then silent knock
Sounds in the houses labour done,
Nor that I'm hollowed out by shock.
O mother heal your son.

The shocks of life come down like blows
Crushing the spirit in us set.
Will helpless attitudes expose
Or find us more triumphant yet?
How may we bear, who feel such grief
Squarely in our hearts, that none,
While others suffer, find relief?
O mother heal your son.

Do not be sad, when this is just.
Justice is the least of me.
My love is more than dust to dust,
And freedom not so free.
But grief like a journey takes us far
Beyond the place where it begun:
My brother's lone exploding star.
O mother heal your son.

Bit by bit he breaks apart.
The speed of light slow motion knows.
The more glorious his heart
The more its quick explosion slows.
Our blood like meteors displayed,
As God is truly three-in-one,
My sister and two brothers prayed:
O mother heal your son.

I prayed that others might explore
My lens of life to see their own
Virulent motives huge as war
Submicroscopic in the bone.
I prayed once more, because I see
Holier than thou, my pride has won
My microbe heart to irony.
O mother heal your son.

Long in the mountains in retreat
With half a life but all my heart,
I heard the sticks of passion beat
My conscience in a cage apart.
Then took a saw and cut some planks,
The sawdust winnowing in the sun,
And built a house in praise and thanks.
O mother heal your son.

Long in the mountains in retreat
I lived this life with all my heart
And touched true peace but found defeat
Taught me the penitence of art,
Drunk in the evenings, there I'd sit
Hallowed (bright fire) by what you'd done.
But no, I could never get used to it.
O mother heal your son.

Back in the city I made my way
Jumbled in tunnels; a million lives
Coming and going; commutable day
The sum of the sacred and secular drives.
Nothing cohered. I felt my mind
Shattered by impact. What had I done?
Life in retreat was making me blind.
O mother heal your son.

The tender traffic of the dawn
Light like love's first certain touch
That instant when a child is born
And praise itself seems nothing much:
Two turtle-doves alone have sung
Such bliss in life, till panics stun.
The flustered parents eat their young.
O mother heal your son.

What ghostly hand my stifled scream
Reached out to soothe through that long night?
It was your own. And then my dream
Broke like an ocean on my sight.
I lay awake and watched the way
The holy family moves as one.
Nor was there anyone to say
O mother heal your son.

Sebastian Barker

By Grand Central Station

By Grand Central Station I sat down and wept
when they said I'd missed the last train to Zion.

They said There's other last trains, take that one standing
like a bull in the pastures of salvation
that's soon to release its cockatrice whistle
and roll in a cough of sulphur to the last
goddam city where you'll see for yourself
the black and white rainbows streaming out
from the last hotel where the horses whinny and flinch,
smelling blood though it's not yet shed; it's at that station
the last just man, the fast-hand angel burdened
with history revenges and love, will step down.

But I was stranded. Prophets were dancing in the streets
crying Dry your appalled appalling tears because nothing
is learned or changes and nothing can be done
and death's a correction in the market.
Try down there a few blocks, there's plenty
of folks in the sky expecting the train to Zion.
So I called to a man of ash as he flew by,
Pardon me – but before he hit the Plaza
he told me No Ma'am I'm sorry,
there never was any scheduled train for Zion.

M.R. Peacocke

Tunes from the Wurlitzer

Back in the time your mam met your dad,
Rob dealt in party favours,
Dehydrated social lubricant.

It crept into corners of his life
Debated decisions, called tunes.
So much funny money
Cash for higher
Chemical, rather than conspicuous, consumption
Clothes and food neglected options
Music an overt apparent expense
Gigs, records, even a jukebox
A proper, stand up, flashing lights,
45 spinning, Happy daze job
The kind Joni stuck a quarter
in when she last saw Richard

As what was enjoyed became relied upon
The product took more of Rob
than he of it, the party people faded.
Good times and social ease left without leaving a note
Only Ben E King and the jukebox stood by him
These days the lubricant is, hydrated , lonely
Conversation confined to the checkout
And the Wurlitzer, lit up,
Hums
Standing by
Unstimulated.

Aidan Halpin

His mouth like the centre of all roses
closes over a mouth not mine

Resuscitation of love, a gasp
of lies heady as musk
drawn into the cavities of past desire.
Unbearable fullness.
Your suave lips count prescribed amounts
before each disengagement,
press out the rhythm of a heart
caged in the near-dead bones of hope.
Your handbook is a half-baked
Kama Sutra translated
with dyslexic penitence
onto sheets of stone.
If only there were more maybes
than today, a shift that splits
but doesn't break apart
what never really was our bed-rock,
the possibility of fault-lines
crazy-paving where small resurrections
might reach out. Thorns and all.

Anne Connolly

12

My heart is eaten by a Dove

A red scratch of skin on the arms of a child
eating oranges; the tear-duct sting of an eye
swollen with blood, mascara and kohl.
Sacred Heart, have mercy on us.

My love-scorched lips are cracked
with thirst and prayer. O Sacred Heart,
have mercy. It is not the mystery of faith
you proclaim; it is the mystery of salvation.

Two shall be in the field; one will be taken.

In this blue nebula of grief I am
born yet again into the bright bitterness
of Barabbas and the wife of Lot, blind-
sighted by stardust, ash and salt.

She turns to look behind her. It is the magic hour,
the first sunlight and the last. My heart
is eaten by a Dove with furnace wings; it's
Your heart that now beats beneath these ribs.

Crista Ermiya

There is a Gentleness Between

There is a gentleness between
the flowing and the ebbing tide:
                    a slack time
when the pull of lunar gravity
takes a breath. Your netted heart
                        flops at rest,
after the tug of breathlessness.
And when knots of the net gently start
to untie themselves, you don't resist;
you trust your trust in gentleness –
forgetting the salt-burn of her lips,
the triumph of thumbprints on your wrists.
And now the tide is so far out
you only hear the sea in your heart.

Liz Loxley

The kelp in amorous coils

The kelp in amorous coils receives
the tide, her gentle talons raking
his silver skin. He for his part veils
his ardour with a slow advance.
Ribbon fingers tendering olives, grapes,
she stretches, languorous, in greeting.

Tide covers kelp, provides
a ceiling mirror. She reclines,
reflects, notes how his features, buried
in her hair, show no emotion;
she writhes with pleasure at his cold caresses,
succumbing to his chilly passion.

When he departs, she, shipwrecked
on the shore, waits in disguise
as bladderwrack, a wrinkled crone,
for their next meeting. She holds her breath,
counts grains of sand and seabirds' cries
till tide relights her fiery heart with ice.

Lyn Moir

Apprehension and the Summer Afternoon

The scene was set wrong that day,
it should have been Baltic.
We should have stood, huddled,
Collars up against the cold
Not listening to the chimes of
The ice cream van while a warm
Breeze stirred my hair.
The sea should have been gun-metal
Bearing winter on its waves,
not sparkling idly.
Fear shimmered in me
as I watched you search my face,
Hands thrust in pockets digging for hope.
It feels like we're over, you said.
You threw the clouds to me then,
settling their grey weight on the sun.
The sea retreated further,
murmuring excuses
I fumbled for denial,
Eyes drawn to the shadow at your back.

Deborah Murray

Gently the wood sorrel and the dove

Evoked wide glades of memory
To shape my quest across the sea,
A world-floor I could float above,
A world-bush filled with scent so fine
Birds lost their minds to music, leaves
Opened to flat plates in the breeze
On which lay food, and coins, and wine.

And from my carpet of wood sorrel
I importuned the gods above
To tell me if these gifts were mine,
Mine to give or mine to take,
Mine to pluck for true love's sake,
Safe in the glade where memory shone,
Where the dove's mate and the flowers had gone,
And where no prize was worth the quarrel.

I ate and drank. My joy was brief.
The coins were folded in the leaf.
I wept, nor slept until I heard
As from a wood, a dove's quiet word,
From herbs, their soothing lullabies.
"Nothing is worth a bean or shred
Compared with what your true love said."
The dove and sorrel closed my eyes.

Sally Evans

Love Still Uproots the heart

the skeleton is a tree
with finger bone branches

look at it as it strokes the tiny children

remembering warmth of skin;
tired of death,

exhausted from all this dying
and being reborn

it reaches between its branches
into the nest

wakes the ruby red bird

nudges from between green leaves
the sleepy bird

J.L.Williams

Propaganda for Sainthood

"Bearers of stigmata frequently exhibit wounds
In accordance with their favourite images of the crucifixion,"
She says, and holds up her hands t'wards me;
I see the light
Right through them.

She asks if I am happy.

Halo'd by attending angels, she offers me:
Rosaries, a knife, a hotel key,
Eucalyptus, myrrh and Virgin Mary candles
Or, at least, take a pamphlet.
She offers me up her sex;

She says she'll love me if it'll make me happy.

But my train is due and I haven't eaten.
Running to my platform,
I request of the sandwich deli:
"Make me one with everything."

I would be happy.

Harlequinade (Alasdair Maloney)

The Smiling Animal at His Appointed Hour

for Andrea Waddell

She died alone, and he – the man who did it –
was grinning as he slithered out the door,
sure he could kill and never be convicted:
could lay blame, in a jury's eyes, on her,
convince them all that some red mist descended
and he, in shock, in panic, couldn't think
beyond his mammal need to be defended.
So mind and body acted out of sync,

or so he'd claim. No countermanding witness
would prove him wrong. The neighbours didn't care:
the best had turned a blind eye to the business;
the worst said, loudly, she should not be there.
And now, she wasn't. He was what they'd wished for,
wasn't he? Did what they couldn't? No:
just took it further. His the hands that killed her.
Theirs the eyes that, smiling, willed it so.

Adam Fish

Love is my Double or Nothing

Above Expectations

I forgot the seedless grapes
and had to do a u turn
on my way back home.

The check-out girl
told me I wasn't allowed
to use my own bag in Aldi Stores.

The sternness of her delivery
and piercing gaze
took possession
of something deep inside.

She was a doppelganger
for Estella in *Great Expectations.*
Love is my double or nothing.

I dropped by again
some weeks later
waiting for a glance.

I became Pip
but wanted to be bolder
than the John Mills version.

I thought, you cannot stop the language of the heart
so I ask her for a one night stanza.
Great Expectations!

Ian Horn

I Contemplate Vaguely the Instruments of Love

I do not like to fuck my lover and stay longer
than I have to. Still, I have the decency to take
a shower before the long sneak home, to use
my regular brand of soap, the kind that hangs from
                                                                a rope.
After the shower, after the liable kiss goodnight,
I drive slowly, the long way round,
dawdle at roundabouts, stop at every light.
Behind the wheel I peel an orange with my teeth,
bathe my hands, my clothes, my face in
                                                                citrus spray.
Home, I kiss my sleeping wife, leave a fruity
smear of cheap deceit upon her hair and cheek
and watch as she sighs and returns to sleep, secure
in the knowledge her trusty hubby is home and safe
                                                                at last.
Then I steal down the hall to the bathroom, wash
my hands and face and dick once more,
sit somewhere in the dark, smoke a cigarette,
contemplate (vaguely) the instruments of love,
while our black cat purrs with tacit knowledge on
                                                                my lap.

Gerard Rudolf

The Ghost-Proof Joke

He is the last among the last. All the acts
who went before have gone before,
the illusionist in clipped moustache and tails,

once favourite of the Prince of Wales,
the stiff-backed tenor from before the war,
the twig-limbed tumblers, the vent act in a mac.

His patter now is blunted like a half-meant curse,
his neutered gags, familiar and cowed,
hang from his brow like matted clumps of hair.

His blarney stone was kissed out in the year
the Crazy Gang surrendered to their crowd.
He has it nailed. It's us that should rehearse.

He is the sum of every screwball turn
there ever was – the pointless cold-war plots,
the powdered egg and snoek, the slipping crown,

the miners' strike and swinging London town.
His routine is the selling out, the national debt,
the ghost-proof joke, the lesson never learned.

Andy Jackson

They intercepted our glances

(Forbidden Love)

They intercepted our glances
caught the way eyes fused
grey meeting blue
noticed our hands touching
saw fingers entwine
just for a moment.

They saw the sparkle
shine of a tear unshed
pink of a blush
on a pale skin
our fragile hearts
waiting to be broken.

Sally James

A passion of tears in the breaking waves

A passion of tears in the breaking waves
in a current of hope her life he saves,
his strength intact he takes her hand
with promise of the safe dry land,
as the tide's cold grip is squeezing tight
he swims her back towards the light.

Once on the sand he builds his castles
to shelter her from painful hassles,
that life has brought from the waters deep
to drown her in no peaceful sleep,
but now away from the ocean spray
he'll keep her safe in every way.

Living in his guarded dunes
she listens to the seagulls' tunes,
and as she feels the dawn's new heat
she knows that she is not complete,
for even though he gives his all
she now must learn her own front crawl.

He holds her tight to say goodbye
he doesn't need to ask her why,
he knows his soul-mate must be free
to save herself inside that sea,
he carries her back reluctance inside
and hands her over to the teary tide.

Hayley Calder

The Rustle of a letter brings me a reprieve

*A rootless person in this alien soil, no sense of belonging. Just another plastic
plant in a painted pot.* Tasilm Nasrin quoted in Captured Voices.

I come from a good home and served
the beast of my country well but now
can't sleep because I'm visited each
night by a man with a noose round
his skinny neck and beard.
I'm part
of the mob that waits almost ashamed
to push the ladder away and watch
the kick and hesitation, the dance,
the way he shits himself and it drips
from his feet to dust, sand and gravel.

A woman mourns for the empty space,
takes the marble body for burial,
hugs the wooden headstone and pushes
it in the ground with a letter to God
begging for a place in paradise.

In my dream I returned home to find
it boarded up, turned into a prison.
Stars rustle like a creaking rope
and there's no one around except me
who's waiting for any sort of reprieve.

Rodney Wood

Set me as a seal upon thine arm, a seal upon thine heart

Oracle

Write my name on your heart;
ink it on your arm. Love

is a tattoo you'll take
to the grave. My burning needle

will sear you, leave you
marked for life, and the dark

that follows after. You
are a hanged man, a drowned man,

nothing worth having in your pockets.
Love alone will illuminate

your skin and save you
from everything you think you are.

Linda France

Remove the outer wrapping
from the box in which
your new lover was delivered.
Carefully detach the polystyrene
packing material – those lightweight scraps
of remaindered dreams and memories
of earlier loves new lovers
always bring with them -
poor dears, they can't help it.
Familiarise yourself with the safety features
of your acquisition, especially the circuit breaker
guarding the core from emotional overload.
You have to build the current up gradually
with this new model. Remember how
the last love failed, spectacularly?
You can't afford a repeat. Study how
Tab A fits Slot B smoothly and firmly.
This is a complex offering, so don't expect
everything optimal at the start. Don't trade in
the minute a feature fails. This sometimes happens
until all working parts are fully bedded in.
Repair, lubricate, nourish, accessorize, add
new components, grow with your lover.
This product does not carry a lifetime guarantee
but it has been designed to give you years of happiness,
and we hope you will be completely satisfied.

Colin Will

I forced my vanity to stand on a cliff...

and it mocked me.

After breathing in the salt sting air
he turns and tells of
my sad nights
where he kept me warm,
oiled my back so rejection would run.

He whispered words to build my ship.
The stern: "Master of my fate."
The bow: "Captain of my soul."
Crafted with some truths
which billowed up to wind the sails
setting me once again upon the sea.

He says.
"You would not rally
had I not shot along your
synapse my well worn refrain
of possibility,
a little intertwined with ideas of destiny."

He laughs, smirks.
He knows for all the threat
we will not push.

Mairi Sharratt

29

The Ruse of Coincidence

The breast is shaped like a teardrop.
The Greeks believed the Amazons sucked its strength
up into their right shoulders.

Words are like teeth:
when one is rotten,
the whole jaw aches.

My body resembles a pear –
a long fruit of white flesh
you sliced into elegant quarters.

Missing breasts. Hard shoulders.
Loose canines. Bruised pears.
                              Oh love,
I'm through with your disguises and conclusions ...

Naomi Foyle

Lot's Wife looking back

Sodom

I understood to look back
meant the end caught
between Lot and a pillar
of salt, the gravity of lust
decided it for me. I could
never live up to his ideals.
And those little girls! I
took it with a pinch,
chose infinite anonymity.
There are worse ends
than this – worse acts.
On a step in Nagasaki
an orphan shadow remains.
Only love is to die for,
each sparkling grain a rock.

Hazel Cameron

A Last Map of Reconstruction

St Ballista's space shot takes its time across no man's land
so you invent stories like hairstyles walking into a ball
past doors of myth; on banana skin floors

An ear hears the veils and mist which rise from sorrow
returned on tales encoded in scrimshaw
sad upon a last leviathan's tooth

I suspect lost worlds and timeslips tremble your mind
tripped on rehearsals spinning through safety nets
gaped in tears and poor repairs

As adobe thoughts turn nomad at the next cantina
a salt song draws cheeks in orders for tequila; for lemons
danced upon the hat of a Mexican memory

A mark left after that which made it has passed
is lonely on your tongue
and young words are fleshless bones of misspelling
and young words are fleshless bones
and young words are fleshless

Ric Hool

The precise geometry of his hand

The Artist said
In the marks we find rhetoric
In the shading we detect truth

Where is the line you draw to draw from me my own diameter?
Butter-licked, cat scratched, fluid-stung, callus marked
Nails trace tensile tolerations of skin

Once, while explaining the etiquette of lay-bys
You made trees disappear behind your thumb
I never understood the lesson, the imparting of wisdom
Less interesting than the toilet break offered.
Your wisdom, indistinct, out of focus...
I remember, still, how October revealed the high nests

Within the talk of statistics,
While inspecting the length of digits,
We uncover suspicions in the topography of palms

The magician said
In the hiding we often reveal
In the showing we often conceal

You once conjured lint from abdominal scar
Extremities that once hid pennies found fortune
There is much to be said for finger theories.

James Oates

The Languorous and Voluptuous Five Senses

The languorous and voluptuous five senses?
But all five senses can't *be* voluptuous
See, hear, smell, touch -
Taste

Lord knows I have enjoyed discovering
The languorous side of those five
With voluptuous others
And certainly the sight
Helped ignite my desire
To divine your sensitive side

And I can touch your voluptuousness,
Taste it, and I can
Do it all languorously
Olfactory senses
Only heighten the tension,
But hearing?

You can't hear voluptuous
When you can hear it
It's a little *past* voluptuous

And how do you listen languorously?

Sophia Walker

The Invisible Ticking of Remorse

It's what I didn't say and now words hang
like those plastic bags in an autumn tree,
veils from missing brides; I know it was wrong
for words to be left between you and me,
as year after year I watched time escape,
and now I know, I didn't say enough.
Like Hardy writing thirty years too late,
scribbling in the dark and cutting-up rough.
Tell me can poetry re-make the past?
Does it have that transforming quality?
Do you have a ready answer to that?
And what can and does it achieve for me?
What I didn't say hurts and the knowing shocks,
I can't balance the books; it's a loss that costs.

Tom Kelly

The Bed Where Love So Often Liberated Us

You breathe heavily while I hold your shoulders
We see eye-to-eye (the first time in years).
The pair of us breathless: me through fear,
you because you're running out of air.

The bed where love so often liberated us,
where reflected in our own deep pools
we saw one person: fused into one person,
has become a vision of sorrow.

In the blank days while you're away
being pieced together, I study
the rings on my hands; one my mother's,
one reminding me we were once alive.

Who will switch the boiler to summertime?
Who will paint the high windowsills, cut the grass,
if you don't come back? I know nothing.
Is this love realised, or just despair?

It takes me five nights of loneliness to cry;
five nights to know that only the naïve
can hope; that this might be our time
to wonder if love is stronger than death.

I don't believe the light nights will return
and every hour you're away is meaningless.
Were I made of wood I'd be beyond love
but I embraced it and it's left me flayed.

When you come back I check you over,
try to visualise your kidneys, your heart.
These past weeks have taken you by the scruff
and I see one body in torture: yours and mine,

dying for love, love which has different laws.
We must learn to lie and savour now;
resign ourselves that it is enough -
it comes for nothing – gives us everything.

Maureen Almond

36

The trap is sprung, and I am in the trap

Caught between the juniper horizon of your arms,
The swan-danced water of your eyes.
Your mosaic smile as it charms
En-cages me in the pearl of your thighs.

The trap is sprung, and I am in the trap-

Wedged between your love and lust,
The placidness of your gentle skin
Completely coated in cosmic dust,
That diffuses from within.

The trap is sprung, and I am in the trap-

Surrounded by your velvet voice of gales,
That curls and loops around my bones.
And your cotton hair that billows and sails,
And your cheeks of cranberry tea scones.

The trap is sprung, and I am in the trap-

Engulfed in the broadness of your chest,
As it merges with the vastness of your back.
As the hearth of your body completely undressed,
Surrounds me in glorious garnet attack.

The trap is sprung, and I am in the trap-

Trapped in your branch like fingers,
In the grasp of your heart's glove.
Your tender presence always lingers
For you've trapped me in your love.

The trap is sprung, and I am in your trap.

Arielle Karro

Do you hear me where I sleep?

Do you hear me where I sleep?
Lungs crackling like an old LP,
everybody cares, nobody understands.
Endless waiting, each day a little worse.
Rings removed from swollen fingers,
ward 15 and blood on the sheets.
Pneumonia, septicaemia,
oxygen dangerously low.
Tongue lolling from your mouth,
plastic tubes and sedation.
A Spanish nurse in ICU.
At the limit of treatment,
on the edge of night.
Stroking your hair,
as you travel beyond fear.
Clinging to your hands,
as you are rescued from guilt and pain.
Inhaling your memory,
exhaling your loss.
Somniloquy of the slumbered.
Do you hear me where I sleep?
She is silent, yet speaks.

Jonathan Glasper

38

In Cold Deliberation

Song of Barbed Wire

I am the great divider.
Before me, was empty space
wide open.

1876, my tips glint silver
in the Texan sun.
I bring the Longhorns up short
in the shade of the Menger
and you are awe-struck.

I've made great strides since
so nothing else can.
I fence off, separate,
call a halt to free-ranging.
I bring order, straight lines
to undulating hills.

Tackle me at your peril.
I will embrace you.
The barbs
of my single twist,
double twist,
concertina coils,
razor wire ribbons,
grip and rip,
tear and maim.
I execute
decisions you make
in cold deliberation.

However much you multiply
I create division.
This is not your land;
this is my land,
every
severed
piece.

Nancy Somerville

Remember I am not Temptation to you

I was not the apple. I did not seduce you
with a serpentine strike. I was not the hands
holding your head on a platter,
nor the hands waving seven multicoloured veils.
We will not be destroyed by fire, ice or flood.
This passion this is everlasting. I know.

We do not give love. We make it
to fill the emptiness and ennui
of monochrome motel rooms.
Do not mistake vacancies
for invitations. Do not suggest
another way to pass the time.
Do not disturb the unrest
of this moment. Love is only
the absence of apathy.

Between pressed lips, locked like couplings,
intertwined between your fingers and mine,
we hold the secret. We've learned
a gold band is not love. We've learned
a hand is meant to touch. We know
the heart is a working muscle
made to beat at the slightest stimulation.

Brittany N. Crosby

The first time I met algebra

my first line of defence was to attack it
with anagrams; but grab ale, a garble, even
bare gal were not enough to cure the trauma.

My former fear was long division-
those Babel-towering numerals spoke
no language that I knew: I was number dumb.

My mathematics were derisory, my thematic
was prosody. No rosy future beckoned me
from the thorny bush of numeracy.

Algorithms gave me the blues.
Quadratics ruled the roots in schools.
Fractions made me fractious.

I was top of the form in despondency
until a classmate reminded me that
x and y are the last two letters of sexy.

So I wrote a sexy poem for her
about how an x wanted to get a y
between satin sheets of parentheses

but I received the same rejection as
my maths exam submission –
were you born stupid, or do you practice?

On my way home from school I noticed
a woman weeping by the railway station.
No need to guess. I knew: my maths teacher.

Eddie Gibbons

Caprice on the Arizona Border

If moonlight is strong enough, cricket played under moonlight
is surely a pastoral caprice; thieves, or bandits, hiding in whites,
under their arms a roll of carpet, mark out the circle of their secret
game, carrying bundles of sticks, two bats, and the famous ruby
ball. Between them a chain of 22 yards laid as sanction across
the Arizona border staking their claim. The teams like ghosts shake
hands. The carpet is unrolled like a prayer mat to the moon. No
sound but the mallet knocking. The stumps aligned and the bails
reverently lowered into their niche. Like Bedouin the players wait
in tents, the desert waits. Someone has drawn in the sand.
The game is silent, just the footfalls as the bowler runs, the tap
tapping of the nocturnal bat and that chord as leather strikes willow.
The desert moon will reflect on the ritual, the deep desire to summon
a field, to lay down the pasture, to anoint the gates, to whistle
up grazing sheep while shepherd boys take turns in the guise
of these exiles, performing for themselves this instructive dance
like insects or birds repeating their song, this ceremony of home.

S.J. Litherland

The cheating cicada arrives to lie

She. She escaped the ward & disappeared with the physician, into the night
With her hair cut longer, gold trapped within it to ward off Egyptians
Her own home, now quiet and moth eaten - alone, her own husband, decaying.

She. She is talked about in church cafes, who is her sweetheart? How is his young
child?
His wife now lost, never knowing when to call him, never knowing the answers
Their once elegant mansion's tainted - its songs trapped within its cocooned walls.

She stands in plastic gloves, tight fitting - halogen light shows her perfect lashes
Arterial red splashes upon her - hands gripping the wires like her life depended on
them
The Fallen angels' chorus erupts from adjoining spaces - synchronised with her
heartbeat.

Stephen James Moore

43

Angels With Sadist Eyes

Midnight has blackened the river to thick tar,
where swans, not moving, certainly not sleeping,
arch their wings white origami angels, dark

space instead of eyes; a moon fractured
its globe forgotten, silvered eel in blank water
somersaulting in some hidden swell

some unseen spasm beneath the anchored
swans, the seeming peace. This river offers
nothing in explanation, no advocate

of comprehension. *This is the beginning
of my life or the end.* I stand on a bridge
at midnight understanding nothing.

Sheila Templeton

Return like Cornered Foxes

By Lisbon docks
I sat down and wept.
By the moorings of a
hundred silver dock-slicing *barcos.*
through short, tight sobs
we haggle sourly.
"Regatear" you murmur,
lowered eyes smeary.

Under a cleanly punctuated
preto sky
you are turning anguish,
our odd *amizade*
into a ridiculous
language lesson.

"O despreza"
I cry, pull at your
sleeve as your curled lip
hurls
"melodrama"
into the balmy *noite.*

Were she to get up now
see us from the *varand,*
I would kiss your lips, drop
your infidel hand as we
return like *raposas encurralados.*
to the *pensão,*
guilt smearing our mouths
like phosphorescence.
Leaking stars.

Carolyn Patricia Richardson

45

a knife is stuck in the engine that pumps my blood

she said and
it makes that juicy sound

standing on a corner in Monterey
torpedo pregnancy
nights under Brooklyn Bridge

he was an instrument
an early amethyst sky
there were never any alternatives
to this way of transcendence

rogues and rascals rose up in front of her
lifted their stolen hats

her garden was a work of art
paths lit with burning torches
rogues and rascals shrieked like hyenas

doctors told her to give up those
high pressures in the heart
am I really old?

fell like a feather in the armchair
holding a phone message
after breakfast

the coffin was small
her rogues and rascals wept all over the slopes
and into the woods

nothing despicable
just glory and sleep now

and that juicy sound

Michael Blackburn

Dragonfly's message under the Linden Tree

Before my father's time no Swedes used last names:
you were your father's son, your father's daughter.
He was a modernist, adopted the new fashion
and the name Linnaeus, after the tree in the rectory garden.

He taught me the names of plants,
scolded me when I forgot them,
so I took mnemonic routes to improve recall,
two words to bring back a phrase
from my mental nebula.

My *System* is based on sex, of course:
how many parts, how arranged,
how positioned? These questions
lead to natural groupings, like with like,
like with similar, and so families are formed.

Under the massive Linden Tree
sugary drops of sap fall from aphids' arses,
attracting ants, wasps, beetles, bugs,
and the bigger beasts that feed on them.
Hornets drone through the branches,
a dozen kinds of bird flutter and pounce,
and the green flashes of hawker dragonflies
zip through summer air, fearsome jaws
clasping hapless victims. I have read the message
of their bodies, and they are classified.

Colin Will

In the Richness of the Red

He picks at the bone
            for no real reason.
An excuse to go.
I respond with words of love.
                Still feel the blow.

I read the guilt in his eyes as he stammers,
                  'Sorry.'
Feel the sting in lip and soul
from this man
            I would marry.

Yes, a million times yes,
I know he would ask,
            if only he were free
but ties, old and new, like fishhooks,
tug his flesh and tear him away.

Can I blame him,
            this charismatic, self-obsessed man,
for inflicting pain?
He is also a victim,
            driving himself insane.

In this match there is no winner.
On that we agree.
Then blood, from my wound,
defiles his upturned face,
            as he kneels before me.

Etta Dunn

The mice squeaked in the housewives' traps

In the darkness of her little house
In the small Mexican *pueblo*
We lay on the too small *cama.*
And she turned her soft face to me
Whispering as though ears pressed against us.

Alice, I have had my rogues and rascals
Now it is you I love, you I trust with my heart, my body.
And we kissed and held each other through the night
While, in outraged disapproval, in every *casa*
The mice squeaked in the housewives' traps.

Carolyn Patricia Richardson

A boy with green eyes and long lashes

Stranger Sex

I slept with a boy with green eyes and long lashes.
Caught in oval frames of longing, an embrace held me
the way spider's web hold rain up to morning.

Rustling, I put on my clothes. My dress chrysalis,
I stepped outdoors and fastened shell buttons to the neck,
wanting not one seed shed by his touch brought to light.

Crows jaded by cloud put on leotards to flip acrobatics
in routine sky, wings flicked through blades of grass,
unpeeled shades of green surrendered to whims of wind.

Moss creep across hand-shaped spaces in my being,
I felt it, a slow grow in the wake of his touch, wet velvet,
somehow living in follicles pricked open by a tongue.

Night loosened its stays, cast ribbon shadows to thread
through afternoons, hillsides slithered with slick snakes.
Summer lifted a calico skirt to show me hermaphrodite day.

Trunks, leaves, clutches -the hard and soft everywhere.
We did not know our sex, I saw that part of female is male.
I couldn't speak, my lips redefined, stone epitaphs to a kiss.

I thought I could leave the moment where I found it.
The boy was gone, but I noticed everything, everything.
It made no sense how it was Genesis, the morning after

someone let there be light. I looked up and down
like people who lived in the dark so long seeing all
that surrounded them, wondering if they'd ever sleep again.

Angela Readman

We wrote our cyphers with anatomy

Our cyphers
that art encrypted
genome be thy key
thy keyword come
thy code be done at birth
as it is in crosswords (6)
give us this day our daily clue
and forgive us our death
as we forgive dissection
and lead us not into enigma
but deliver us from answers
for thine is the body and the data and its organs
indefinitely replicated
myqz (4)

Colin Donati

an accidental picturesqueness

I inhabit a minute impossible to second-guess before
the hilltop, where my eyes first catch precise angles

between goat and stream and boulder, intelligently designed,
artificially stung to order, while blogging ASDA mums debate

the latest party leaders' election debacle and Xerox,
once synonymous with photocopying, market a rash

of office products from an immaculate website. I know only
an accidental picturesqueness links the nature scene,

Kylie from Wiltshire's verdict of 'lol', my urge to buy
ASDA, to xerox my backside, but everything makes sense

even when the goat drops beneath the boulder. Is it dead?
Clarity assumes permanence, as it did yesterday in passing.

Rob A. Mackenzie

Into the redwoods brooding

The blurred heart still visible on the trunk
of the veteran beech in Brusselton Woods
as it sprouts new leaves like green mayday flags
ahead of the tardy bluebells
I take as a good sign. Years ago
in another wood, consumed by flames,
I melted like a candle. Lost my shape,
no longer fitted for the life that waited.

This woman, patient in her old coat
is content to stand, watch the blue tits
mate mid air above the fallen oak,
its roots visible like arteries in a post mortem.
I lean against it, feel its uneven skin.
You fill sacks with leaf mould,
your hands inside the earth
coaxing rich clods to the surface.

As we make our way back to the car,
we inhale the forest smells, crouch
to catch the perfume of a primrose
see wood anemones nod pale heads
the breeze still chill after this long winter.
I hold your muddy hand, drawing its warmth,
feel the blood pump
through the veins in your wrist.

Jo Colley

Your Skin Will Outlive You

Do you know that your skin will outlive you?

My mother's, before they made me
Leave her, smelled so good against my face,
Like a baby's, purged of all impurity through her
Long dying: I didn't know then, it was still alive.

Whether the brain, like hers, dies first, killing
The breath, and with it, the heart: or like my father's,
Holds out until the struggling, suddenly blood-starved
Heart gives up, strangling brain, then breath:
Either way, the rest follows, bowels, liver, kidneys,

Until there's just skin, holding things together
In its quiet way for a day or two more, mute
Witness of our premature grief, the attendant's
Wash cloth, the clutching hands of the bereaved.

No-one told her skin it was time to be dead.
When I let her go for the last time, maybe
It registered, somehow, my hand on her arm.
Left alone, perhaps it was still
Anticipating the heaven of actual touch.

Valerie Laws

The Moons that Rise and Set Unused

MacAdam's First Act of Environmental Courage

Shortcutting down a darkened close,
MacAdam finds the past year's
unused moons wheelie-binned outside
the back door of a dealership —
moons for howling or winching by,
moons for fishing out of gutter dubs
on a Friday night, moons that sing
a song about I love you, moons
made of Wensleydale, papier mâché
or silver paint, moons of understated beauty
and moons with a faulty connection
to the motherboard.
                          Aware there are no
local facilities for lunar recyclate,
MacAdam opens his pockets
to jostle the lot in among the detritus
he's gathered —
                          the unheard knocking
of a pantomime horse, a portrait
of the author as an official demand
for chocolate, and the unknown
comedian's failed last laugh —
                          thinking:
If all that reflected light
was landfilled, everyone would see
just how much was going to waste.

Andrew Philip

If you do me the wrong of thinking I am beautiful

If you do me the wrong of thinking I am beautiful
and consider that a compliment,
you're adding insult to injury –
worse, restricting yourself to cliché:
second-hand language, pallid imagery.

Do you really believe it's possible to know
everything that there is to know about me
simply by looking?
Listen, that's the only way
to complete comprehension.

Is more revealed by the mirror
or in another person's gaze?
How can you ever be clever enough to know
whether it's better to be beautiful or bright.
Or beautiful enough not to care?

As for the influence of other people,
friends, family; perfect strangers. Huh.
Thank goodness for a second chance
to eliminate that first impression.
But do you really imagine this is going to work?

Carole Baldock

56

The Exact Measurements of my Captivity

The ship's bow splits open, her vaginal
darkness gaping as if a gravedigger's spade
had sliced apart crusted turf
exposing the infinite black.

We enter the lower deck slowly
filing from frosted clarity into cloying darkness
the elemental smells of metal and oil
thick on our tongues, filling our throats.

Last on, I feel the rumble as if earth was thundering
down on wood. I turn, like Lot's wife, to see
the metallic labia shiver shut, drawing closed
on all that was, swallowing us deep and wholly.

We pull away from the shore
trailing our wavering umbilici.
Below us the ocean's mighty roar
and below that the hard black rock
and below that the red fire, the red red fire
at the earth's core.

Alison Flett

Carry a legend like a banner

First come the small, betraying details:
a chaotic fifth column, still open to question;
an unruly rabble of matters of fact.

One thing's for certain, we fell in love,
against all the odds, in spite of ourselves;
we agreed on that much in the end.

The unvarnished truth doesn't last, of course;
it's embellished and polished and streamlined
as the water pours endlessly under the bridge.

But the story goes: we fell in love,
against the day and despite ourselves;
we only argued about the bitter end.

Even if it's only a flag of convenience,
representing something greater than yourself,
you should carry a legend like a banner.

The rumour is, we fell from grace;
against the grain, to spite ourselves,
we arrived at the end of the line.

The fog of myth is all that's left
once the battle for the truth is finally lost and
the tattered colours are running away.

Andrew J. Wilson

Returning homeward through a land I love like a lover

Home... where is home? Not the place where you 're born
Nor where you passed your earliest years.
They're more like family. You grew with them.

It took me half a lifetime but I found my love.
Fell for its ruined beauty and its soul -
Quarries like Roman theatres,
Scarred valleys in between the flower-clad hills,
The mingling scent of lavender and pines.

I've plucked its fruits and bled upon its spines.
And now I know this land - intimately.
I entered it at every orifice,
Crawled deep inside its glittering crystal bowels,
Lighted its flooded tunnels with my torch
Marvelling at its cavernous spaces.
Touching the surface wasn't enough for me.

Fiona Pitt-Kethley

A Golden Oriel in the Orchard

They're hard to spot even when you're not
weeping. Shy and high-flying, they offer only
a flash of yellow within the canopy green. A crick
comes with the territory, unless you're on apple-picking
ladders, but then you'd scare the bird.

But with tears – particularly those that blur the mind's
eye, when you're on a bench near a station, say, or
looking along the line of carriages, and memories are
stirred of that last picnic beneath the ripening Granny
Smiths – it's easy to lose your ornithological
perspicacity. It's easy to confuse one with a *Bullock's*, or
a *Hooded*, or, more likely – if you've got a song driving
you to distraction – Hoagy Carmichael's *Baltimore*.

Afterwards you could kick yourself, at the twitchers'
convention, when you pick up your tote bag
and pin on your society button, and with the upset
receding down the track, you swap lists of recent
sightings, including the *Golden* you saw or kind of saw
among the apple trees of your mind, and that know-all
from the Audubon says surely you mean *icterus spurius*,
the *Orchard*, because the *Golden's* never been spotted in
North America. That is mortifying enough, but then
he points out: "And it's oriole, not oriel. An oriel
is a small room with a polygonal window." And
once again you sit down and weep.

Alistair Robinson

The very word love offends with its nudity.

Like a mist it descends over the lovers.

Their bed is green,
they can only feel, hear, taste and smell
the other's presence,
until it clears,
and a black rainbow appears.

Like a crystal of snow, formed in icy ether,
perfect in symmetry,
terrifying in fragility,
then a moment of heat, and it melts,
into the comfort
of black slush.

Etta Dunn

Jokes in Bombed effigies

The Arcship

Three decades into a century sleep excursion
Deep in ink darkness of velveteen void
Star travellers awake reluctantly to clarion distress signal
Blue planet beneath archship a cacophony of shortwave radio emissions
Clumsy, cluttered satellites choking orbital space
The starlost weep in complex chemical empathy, powerless
As the madding crowds below topple the statue of the last dictator
Lizard brainstems stimulated violently, paying homage to the prophet
Defending love with fear and hatred, burnt fists and bloody hair
These strange creatures make meaningless his effortless messages
Their cartoonists scribble to tell jokes in bombed effigies
Everywhere the smoke of burning crude pollutes blue ozone
Primates savagely set light to ancient buildings,Gleeful and gleaming
Eyes wild with the raw necessity of resource conflict
The arcship hangs majestically beyond the dark side of the planet's moon
Sending information-rich pink lasers through selected cortexes
To inspire obedience in those monkeys most open to revelation
But sigh quietly, desperately as the crowds revel at a wise man's crucifixion
They murmur the word over and over: religion, religion
The species' sad, reflective songs lost in the brutal ire of armies marching
Of rough gangs arming themselves with rocks and broken furniture
Customised farm implements and ploughshares beaten into jagged swords
Every single book burnt to repel the harsh, hungry winter's chill
The suffering sighs of heat-exhausted infants, belly-swollen with starvation
Watching the last dying embers of imagination, so complex recede back
into ignoble instinct irretrievable. The travellers watch the decline of the bell curve
Such waste, they sigh, so strange, so strange unable to react to this mass self-extinction
Perpetually perplexed by such rapid cultural change
Within the shared culture below which can only communicate subjectively:
While they sleep mind-to-mind curled tight in amniotic chambers
Blissfully ignorant in their enlightenment, isolated
The arcship guides them towards the next carbon-based species
Hoping that perhaps this time they will awaken soon enough to make a difference
If they can just cover the distance make sense of the madness, the violence, the guns
Before culture consumes itself inevitably, voraciously
An unfeeling black hole consuming infant suns.

Texture (Bram Gieben)

Old Gold on the October Trees

(for Colin Donati)

You text and then phone,
a dream of mice and autumn,
your bedroom fall.

Empty traps luring tiny hearts.

I tell you to *bait them with cornflakes.*
You are a gentle, determined hunter,
Muddled and over thinking everything,

worrying the sun from the sky,
decanting buckets of mice to the links,
the old gold from the October Trees.

I dreamt of leaves you said

although I realise in the cold
breakfast of morning
they might be cornflakes.

Kevin Cadwallender

All Cries are lost in the confusion of storms

The Wind's Song

It rises from the sea
over rooftops
between lanes
across fields.

It throws me against the fence post
like an impatient lover,
flattens me onto the hard surface
of wood.

              I snap a few moments in my camera.

It paints the landscape:
Sea – bottle green
Breakers – white
Shoreline – brown
              dark
                blurred.

Waves lash over the paved edge,
hands reaching to take something back...

I turn from the shore
hold onto walls
hide in doorways
duck into lanes.

Inside, the song continues,
a murmur of flagstones
wet, creeping in.

Nalini Paul

I look homeward now and melt

I look homeward now and melt. For all my dancing on
the horizon's sharp, far edge of madness, the white
blossom in the orchard is singing sweeter love-songs.
The wild earth is putting out vines that wind around my
feet like snakes and my hands pause as I reach to tear
them clear. For all that I called myself 'messenger,' for
all that I flew in majestic, dazzling spirals of mad and
wondrous light... Home remains, whispering as I turn
and turn and turn in the delightful gyre of space.

I look homeward now and melt towards the evening
fireside, to the tangled gardens of memory... To the
orchards I have never truly known and the shooting star
beyond the garden's edge...

The swallows call me. The eagle, the hawk and the gulls.
The wind is rising and flying will be as keen and sharp
as glass...

But, I look homeward now and melt; I flow towards the
dreams of my kin. Like a spell, some earthy *glam* of
hope; like sweet wine on tired lips and the soil of home
on my hands. It is a magic too dense for the air. I lie on
the soft green grass and close my eyes to flying.

I look homeward now and melt into the sweet
blossoming heart of my home on the heavenly Earth.

The swallows and the eagle and the hawk and the gulls
fly on in the gathering storm of their element, while I
rest, at last, in mine.

Tom Coyopa

65

An Illicit Kiss Might be Forming

You took all
the yellow pills:
destroyed the place.

I took eight
flights of stairs
to escape,

find myself
breathing
on the old flat roof

with a *How To* book
and a juicy man
with a colossal tongue.

Kathleen Kenny

History from his old wounds

extract from Command to Forget

All the lives lived, all the devilish spurnings,
the haywire of secrets, the kelp of shame and
thoughts no man should have in bible hours.

You might write your name there in the dust
on the blade of the chisel of God, the ten slabs
stilled in lost silence beneath the mercy seat.

All the palaces of small mercies pillaged;
in the ruins wags a book of wiving strategies,
the new skin skidding round the old chicanes.

You make swatches of your memory, where
absence foils limit, break-up foils bounce,
your annals in ravenous, sulphurous bigtime.

All those wounds and woundings, drolleries
of the unborn, apostolic effigy, carbon copy
threats, all the clipped ransom notes to self.

You were no mere skimming, no off-scouring,
not a sweeping, but nor did you equal a star;
you're a trimming, a peg in the chronicle's bag.

All the tiny earlies: creeping myrtle, creeping
phlox and squill rolling back in tidal duty.
All the nubbins. All the velvety advancers.

You could do what you can to show you can,
grapple the archetypes, raze the watchtower,
run its length before it falls upon your faith.

All the lights fussed up - flint and bow drill,
iliou persis, Pharos, Menlo Park, the glare
that dizzies as you gad in your glasshouse.

You tend to notice that you are not in a room
until the light is on. Impasse... Zugzwang...
then laid down by the last of your humility.

All these starlight pourings from stigmata -
what is their history is our arcana, our cant,
our winking chintz; our sob story their lore.

You marry the tideline - it is more matched
by chance than what we call back story,
its frontier mapped with disappointments.

Roddy Lumsden

The Conundrum into Damnation

"And Spring brought the idiots' frightful laughter..."
-Rimbaud

They've reinvented our gods at Saint Christopher Street.
The downtown side.
Funny, it all looks the same.
Saint Vincent stopped taking the damned,
the market will handle them now.
If I walk the street where I once loved Blondie,
she can no longer be found.
Instead: jackals who'll swear they've seen the face of the deity.
To love you I had to leave.
Funny, it all 'looks' the same.
I made it there.
Now the love is genuine.
Funny, the looks, a state of mind.

Martin Belk